FOREVER FRIENDS

. . .

A Keepsake of
Questions and Answers
for Best Friends

chartwell
books

This Journal Belongs To:

. . . .

&

. . . .

FRIENDS SINCE

. . . .

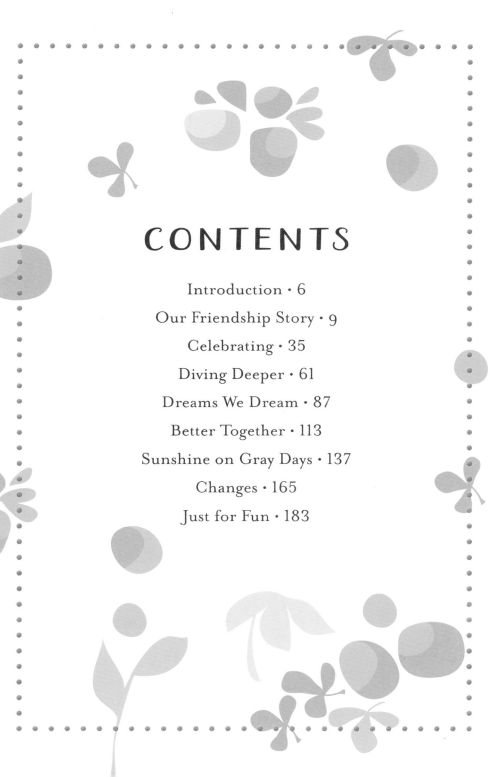

CONTENTS

INTRODUCTION

BEST FRIENDS FOREVER

Your best friend is the one who loves you at your core, the first person you call when you have awesome news and the one you reach out to when you're worried or sad. Through it all you've had some pretty great times—you've laughed, you've cried. And laughed again ... and again!

In the pages of this journal you'll find fun quizzes, creative prompts, and dozens of thoughtful questions that invite you to remember the amazing times you've had together and build on your forever friendship. And by journaling together you'll create an incredible keepsake as you write about each other, yourselves, and the extraordinary friendship you've formed.

HOW TO USE THIS JOURNAL

There is no right or wrong way to use this journal. Work straight through or jump around. Answer all the questions or only the ones that speak to you both. Take the prompts in a new direction, if you like, and add your own questions. Color, doodle, underline, draw arrows and exclamation points.

Each friend is assigned a different color flower—a gray star or yellow flower. Write your thoughts on the page where you see your flower.

ME = ☆   YOU = ✿

Some of the prompts are light and fun, designed for you to answer quickly. Other questions ask for deeper reflection, encouraging you to think about what you want from your friendship and from life, and to understand how your bestie thinks about those same questions. The most important "rule" is this: Have fun and express yourself.

Let's get journaling!

OUR FRIENDSHIP STORY

Best friends are there for each other no matter what, helping to weather life's storms and navigate waters both choppy and calm. Celebrate your special bond and explore what friendship means to you both.

Describe the day you knew we would become friends:

....
....
....
....
....
....
....
....
....
....
....
....

How did you know?

....
....
....
....
....
....
....
....
....
....
....
....
....
....

Describe the day you knew we would become friends:

How did you know?

In what ways does your BFF have your back?

1

2

3

4

5

6

In what ways does your BFF have your back?

1

2

3

4

5

6

We first met at . . .

....
....

We were ⬚ years old. I remember that you . . .

....
....
....
....
....
....
....
....

I never thought that . . .

....
....
....
....
....
....
....
....
....
....
....
....

We first met at . . .

....

....

We were [   ] years old. I remember that you . . .

....

....

....

....

....

....

....

....

I never thought that . . .

....

....

....

....

....

....

....

....

....

....

....

What is one thing your best friend has done
for you that you will never forget?

What is one thing your best friend has done
for you that you will never forget?

How do you think your BFF would describe you?
Do you agree with that portrayal?

How do you think your BFF would describe you?
Do you agree with that portrayal?

Draw or write positive words or images in the space below that
describe how you see your best friend.

Draw or write positive words or images in the space below that describe how you see your best friend.

HOW WELL DO YOU KNOW YOUR BESTIE?

TAKE THE QUIZ, THEN CHECK EACH OTHER'S ANSWERS!

MIDDLE NAME:

BIRTHDAY:

FEATURE OR BODY
PART YOUR FRIEND IS
MOST PROUD OF:

FAVORITE CANDY:

CELEBRITY CRUSH:

CHORE YOUR FRIEND
ABSOLUTELY HATES:

ONE THING YOUR
BFF WOULD CHANGE
ABOUT THE WORLD:

FAVORITE MOVIE:

FIRST NAMES OF
YOUR FRIEND'S
PARENTS:

BIGGEST FEAR:

HOW WELL DO YOU KNOW YOUR BESTIE?

TAKE THE QUIZ, THEN CHECK EACH OTHER'S ANSWERS!

MIDDLE NAME:

BIRTHDAY:

FEATURE OR BODY PART YOUR FRIEND IS MOST PROUD OF:

FAVORITE CANDY:

CELEBRITY CRUSH:

CHORE YOUR FRIEND ABSOLUTELY HATES:

ONE THING YOUR BFF WOULD CHANGE ABOUT THE WORLD:

FAVORITE MOVIE:

FIRST NAMES OF YOUR FRIEND'S PARENTS:

BIGGEST FEAR:

Do you ever compare yourself with your friend?

. . . .

. . . .

. . . .

. . . .

. . . .

. . . .

. . . .

. . . .

. . . .

. . . .

. . . .

What does your bestie do better than you? Where do you shine?

. . . .

. . . .

. . . .

. . . .

. . . .

. . . .

. . . .

. . . .

. . . .

. . . .

. . . .

Do you ever compare yourself with your friend?

....
....
....
....
....
....
....
....
....
....
....
....

What does your bestie do better than you? Where do you shine?

....
....
....
....
....
....
....
....
....
....
....
....
....
....

You're creating an ad to publicize your friend's outstanding qualities.
What will the headline be?

....
....
....
....
....
....
....
....

What are your friend's best points?

....
....
....
....
....
....
....
....

How will you present your BFF?

....
....
....
....
....
....
....

You're creating an ad to publicize your friend's outstanding qualities.
What will the headline be?

....

....

....

....

....

....

What are your friend's best points?

....

....

....

....

....

....

....

How will you present your BFF?

....

....

....

....

....

....

....

What has been the best moment of your friendship so far?

....
....
....
....
....
....
....
....
....
....
....
....

What made that time so special?

....
....
....
....
....
....
....
....
....
....
....
....
....

What has been the best moment of your friendship so far?

What made that time so special?

What's your number-one rule for friendships?

Write a quote that inspires you.

Who do you look up to? Why?

When are you at your most productive?

Where do you go when you want to be alone?

What is your most prized possession?

Celebrating

Life's a party—don't
forget to celebrate!
From cherished
holiday traditions to
birthdays to the small
moments you treasure
together, record
and share the
special times.

Describe the best party you and your bestie have ever attended together.
What made it such a blast?

....
....
....
....
....
....
....
....
....
....
....
....
....
....
....
....
....
....
....
....
....
....
....
....
....
....
....

Describe the best party you and your bestie have ever attended together. What made it such a blast?

Write about your favorite holiday tradition.
What are the sights, smells, and sounds of the day?

....
....
....
....
....
....
....
....
....
....
....

Does your friend celebrate too?

....
....
....
....
....
....
....
....
....
....
....
....
....
....

Write about your favorite holiday tradition.
What are the sights, smells, and sounds of the day?

Does your friend celebrate too?

What rituals, inside jokes, made-up words, or pet phrases
do you and your best friend have?

....
....
....
....
....
....
....
....
....
....
....

How does your "secret language" cement your friendship?

....
....
....
....
....
....
....
....
....
....
....
....
....

What rituals, inside jokes, made-up words, or pet phrases
do you and your best friend have?

....
....
....
....
....
....
....
....
....
....
....
....
....

How does your "secret language" cement your friendship?

....
....
....
....
....
....
....
....
....
....
....
....
....
....
....

HOW WELL DO YOU KNOW YOUR BESTIE?

TAKE THE QUIZ, THEN CHECK EACH OTHER'S WORK!

FAVORITE SEASON:

THE HOLIDAY YOUR
BESTIE LOVES MOST:

FAN OF SURPRISES—
YES OR NO:

BEST GIFT EVER
RECEIVED:

FAVORITE FLAVOR
FOR A BIRTHDAY
CAKE:

MOST DREADED
HOLIDAY TRADITION:

OVER-THE-TOP
DECORATIONS—
YES OR NO:

FAVORITE
CELEBRATORY MEAL:

TOP CHOICE FOR
A PARTY VENUE:

FAVORITE
BIRTHDAY MEMORY:

HOW WELL DO YOU KNOW YOUR BESTIE?

TAKE THE QUIZ, THEN CHECK EACH OTHER'S WORK!

FAVORITE SEASON:

THE HOLIDAY YOUR
BESTIE LOVES MOST:

FAN OF SURPRISES—
YES OR NO:

BEST GIFT EVER
RECEIVED:

FAVORITE FLAVOR FOR
A BIRTHDAY CAKE:

MOST DREADED
HOLIDAY TRADITION:

OVER-THE-TOP
DECORATIONS—
YES OR NO:

FAVORITE
CELEBRATORY MEAL:

TOP CHOICE FOR
A PARTY VENUE:

FAVORITE
BIRTHDAY MEMORY:

How do you celebrate special moments?

....
....
....
....
....
....
....
....
....
....
....
....

Write about a time you had a big win and what you did to mark the occasion.

....
....
....
....
....
....
....
....
....
....
....
....
....
....
....

How do you celebrate special moments?

Write about a time you had a big win and what you did to mark the occasion.

What is the best gift your friend has ever given you?

....
....
....
....
....
....
....
....
....
....
....
....

Why was it so special to you?

....
....
....
....
....
....
....
....
....
....
....
....
....
....

What is the best gift your friend has ever given you?

....
....
....
....
....
....
....
....
....
....
....
....

Why was it so special to you?

....
....
....
....
....
....
....
....
....
....
....
....

FILL THIS GRATITUDE JAR WITH REASONS YOU ARE THANKFUL FOR YOUR BFF!

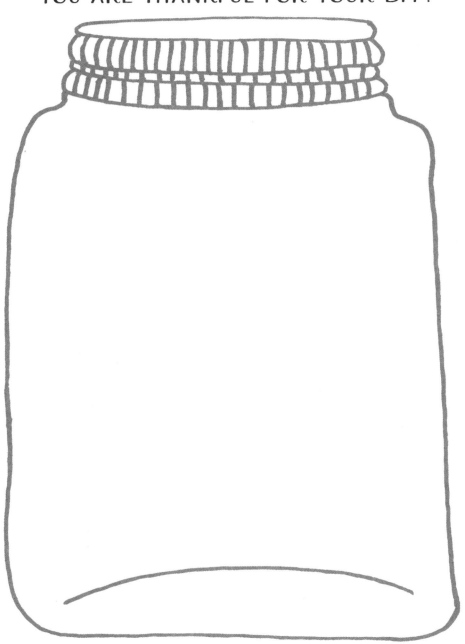

FILL THIS GRATITUDE JAR WITH REASONS YOU ARE THANKFUL FOR YOUR BFF!

Do you love celebrating your birthday? Why or why not?

....
....
....
....
....
....
....
....
....
....
....
....

Share some special birthday memories through the years.

....
....
....
....
....
....
....
....
....
....
....
....
....

Do you love celebrating your birthday? Why or why not?

Share some special birthday memories through the years.

What little victories can you celebrate in everyday life?

....

....

....

....

....

....

....

....

....

....

....

....

Make a list of small accomplishments that you and
your friend can mark together.

....

....

....

....

....

....

....

....

....

....

....

....

....

What little victories can you celebrate in everyday life?

Make a list of small accomplishments that you and
your friend can mark together.

The holiday song that makes me think of you is . . .

....
....
....

Because . . .

....
....
....

I remember that one summer vacation we . . .

....
....
....

One night we stayed out so late that . . .

....
....
....

The most embarrassing thing I've ever done at a party is . . .

....
....
....
....
....
....

The holiday song that makes me think of you is . . .

....
....
....

Because . . .

....
....
....

I remember that one summer vacation we . . .

....
....
....

One night we stayed out so late that . . .

....
....
....

The most embarrassing thing I've ever done at a party is . . .

....
....
....
....
....

If you had no obligations for an entire summer, how would you
choose to spend it?

....
....
....
....
....
....
....
....
....
....
....
....

Plan the ideal summer day.

....
....
....
....
....
....
....
....
....
....
....
....
....
....

If you had no obligations for an entire summer, how would you choose to spend it?

....
....
....
....
....
....
....
....
....
....
....

Plan the ideal summer day.

....
....
....
....
....
....
....
....
....
....
....
....

What future celebrations do you look forward to?

How will you honor graduations, weddings, work promotions, and more with your best friend?

What future celebrations do you look forward to?

....
....
....
....
....
....
....
....
....
....
....
....

How will you honor graduations, weddings, work promotions,
and more with your best friend?

....
....
....
....
....
....
....
....
....
....
....
....
....
....

DIVING DEEPER

No matter how much you think you know about each other, there's always more to learn! Get meaningful insights into your own inner workings and those of your bestie with these thoughtful questions.

How would your relationship be different if your friend were your sister or brother rather than your BFF?

....
....
....
....
....
....
....
....
....
....
....
....

Do you think you would be closer or not as close?

....
....
....
....
....
....
....
....
....
....
....
....

How would your relationship be different if your friend were your sister or brother rather than your BFF?

Do you think you would be closer or not as close?

Are you an optimist or a pessimist?

....
....
....
....
....
....
....
....
....
....
....

How does your outlook affect the way you relate to others,
including your BFF?

....
....
....
....
....
....
....
....
....
....
....
....
....

Are you an optimist or a pessimist?

How does your outlook affect the way you relate to others,
including your BFF?

My first memory of you is . . .

....

....

....

....

....

....

....

I'll always remember the time we . . .

....

....

....

....

....

....

....

One thing we should never do again is . . .

....

....

....

....

....

....

....

My first memory of you is . . .

I'll always remember the time we . . .

One thing we should never do again is . . .

Do you believe in fate?

....
....
....
....
....
....
....
....
....
....
....

Do you think we were destined to become friends?

....
....
....
....
....
....
....
....
....
....
....
....

Do you believe in fate?

Do you think we were destined to become friends?

1 - - - - - - - TO - - - - - - 10

1	2	3	4	5	6	7	8	9	10	TREASURE HUNTS
1	2	3	4	5	6	7	8	9	10	SPICY FOOD
1	2	3	4	5	6	7	8	9	10	COUNTRY MUSIC
1	2	3	4	5	6	7	8	9	10	BARRETTES
1	2	3	4	5	6	7	8	9	10	WATER SKIING
1	2	3	4	5	6	7	8	9	10	COCONUT
1	2	3	4	5	6	7	8	9	10	SALT LAMPS
1	2	3	4	5	6	7	8	9	10	INSECTS
1	2	3	4	5	6	7	8	9	10	SIDE HAIR PART
1	2	3	4	5	6	7	8	9	10	BLACK LICORICE
1	2	3	4	5	6	7	8	9	10	HAUNTED HOUSES
1	2	3	4	5	6	7	8	9	10	CILANTRO
1	2	3	4	5	6	7	8	9	10	VINYL RECORDS
1	2	3	4	5	6	7	8	9	10	MILLENNIAL PINK
1	2	3	4	5	6	7	8	9	10	TOFU
1	2	3	4	5	6	7	8	9	10	FANNY PACKS

RATE THE FOLLOWING THINGS ON A SCALE OF ONE TO TEN, WITH TEN BEING MOST LIKED AND ONE BEING LEAST LIKED. COMPARE YOUR ANSWERS.

1 2 3 4 5 6 7 8 9 10	TREASURE HUNTS
1 2 3 4 5 6 7 8 9 10	SPICY FOOD
1 2 3 4 5 6 7 8 9 10	COUNTRY MUSIC
1 2 3 4 5 6 7 8 9 10	BARRETTES
1 2 3 4 5 6 7 8 9 10	WATER SKIING
1 2 3 4 5 6 7 8 9 10	COCONUT
1 2 3 4 5 6 7 8 9 10	SALT LAMPS
1 2 3 4 5 6 7 8 9 10	INSECTS
1 2 3 4 5 6 7 8 9 10	SIDE HAIR PART
1 2 3 4 5 6 7 8 9 10	BLACK LICORICE
1 2 3 4 5 6 7 8 9 10	HAUNTED HOUSES
1 2 3 4 5 6 7 8 9 10	CILANTRO
1 2 3 4 5 6 7 8 9 10	VINYL RECORDS
1 2 3 4 5 6 7 8 9 10	MILLENNIAL PINK
1 2 3 4 5 6 7 8 9 10	TOFU
1 2 3 4 5 6 7 8 9 10	FANNY PACKS

What's your favorite guilty pleasure?

....
....
....
....
....
....
....
....
....
....
....
....

Why is it a good escape?

....
....
....
....
....
....
....
....
....
....
....
....
....

What's your favorite guilty pleasure?

Why is it a good escape?

What's a good title for the theme song of your friendship?
What would the music genre be?

☆

❀

Write the opening lyrics.

☆

❀

Our best talks center around . . .

Do you consider yourself to be religious or spiritual?

....
....
....
....
....
....
....
....
....
....
....
....
....
....

How does your faith (or lack of it) impact your friendship?

....
....
....
....
....
....
....
....
....
....
....
....
....
....

Do you consider yourself to be religious or spiritual?

How does your faith (or lack of it) impact your friendship?

5 Things We Have in Common:

1.

2.

3.

4.

5.

1.

2.

3.

4.

5.

5 Ways We Are Different:

1.

2.

3.

4.

5.

1.

2.

3.

4.

5.

List 10 little-known facts about yourself.

★ 1.
2.
3.
4.
5.
6.
7.
8.
9.
10.

❀ 1.
2.
3.
4.
5.
6.
7.
8.
9.
10.

Then write 10 about your best friend.

1.
2.
3.
4.
5.
6.
7.
8.
9.
10.

1.
2.
3.
4.
5.
6.
7.
8.
9.
10.

What skill does your BFF have that you most appreciate?

....
....
....
....
....
....
....
....
....
....
....
....

How does it complement your own skill set?

....
....
....
....
....
....
....
....
....
....
....
....
....

What skill does your BFF have that you most appreciate?

How does it complement your own skill set?

What is one thing only your best friend knows about you? (Shhhhhh!)

What is one thing only your best friend knows about you? (Shhhhhh!)

FRIENDSHIP BUILDERS

MAKE A [✓] CHECKMARK NEXT TO EACH THING
YOU'D LIKE TO TRY. IF YOU'D BOTH LIKE TO DO THE
ACTIVITY, MARK IT IN THE "SHARE" COLUMN.

	☆	SHARE	☀
SET ASIDE TECH-FREE TIME			
GO TO A MUSEUM TOGETHER			
TALK ABOUT CHALLENGING TOPICS			
READ YOUR FRIEND'S FAVORITE BOOK AND DISCUSS IT			
SPEND A WHOLE SUNDAY TOGETHER			
TALK ABOUT YOUR FAMILIES AND YOUR PAST			
DO A PROJECT AS A TEAM (BUILD SOMETHING, VOLUNTEER, ETC.)			
COOK OR BAKE SOMETHING TOGETHER			
HAVE A SLEEPOVER			
LEARN SOMETHING NEW TOGETHER			

DREAMS WE DREAM

Break open the limits and let your imagination soar as you think through what-if questions and consider your deepest longings. Share your passions and your dreams with your BFF to bring you closer and recognize what you really want out of life.

Is there something you've always dreamed of doing that you haven't done yet?

....
....
....
....
....
....
....
....
....
....
....

What is standing in your way?

....
....
....
....
....
....
....
....
....
....
....

Is there something you've always dreamed of doing that you haven't done yet?

What is standing in your way?

You can spend one day as your BFF; what is the day like?

....
....
....
....
....
....
....
....
....
....
....
....

Describe it from morning until you go to bed at night.

....
....
....
....
....
....
....
....
....
....
....
....
....

You can spend one day as your BFF; what is the day like?

Describe it from morning until you go to bed at night.

When was the last time you tried something new? What was it?

How did the experience make you feel?

When was the last time you tried something new? What was it?

How did the experience make you feel?

Fill in the following lines with whatever comes to mind.

1. I WANT TO

2. I THINK

3. I LOVE

4. I NEED

5. I DON'T

6. I NEVER

7. I ENJOY

8. I SHOULD

9. I WAIT FOR

10. I AM

Fill in the following lines with whatever comes to mind.

1. I WANT TO

2. I THINK

3. I LOVE

4. I NEED

5. I DON'T

6. I NEVER

7. I ENJOY

8. I SHOULD

9. I WAIT FOR

10. I AM

What new adventure would you like to try with your best friend?

What new adventure would you like to try with your best friend?

If you could travel anywhere in the world, where would
you choose to go? Why?

....
....
....
....
....
....
....
....
....
....
....

What's the first thing you would do when you arrived?

....
....
....
....
....
....
....
....
....
....
....
....

If you could travel anywhere in the world, where would
you choose to go? Why?

....
....
....
....
....
....
....
....
....
....
....

What's the first thing you would do when you arrived?

....
....
....
....
....
....
....
....
....
....
....
....
....
....

CIRCLE YOUR ANSWER THEN COMPARE WITH YOUR FRIEND.

WOULD YOU RATHER...

Have a **MERMAID TAIL** or **FAIRY WINGS**?

Go **SURFING** or **SOAK IN A HOT TUB**?

Have a **CLOAK OF INVISIBILITY** or
the **ABILITY TO READ MINDS**?

Explore the **DEEP SEA** or **OUTER SPAC**e?

Play a **VILLAIN** or a **HERO** in a film?

Marry someone very **WEALTHY** or very **GOOD-LOOKING**?

Time-travel 50 years into **THE FUTURE**
or 50 years into **THE PAST**?

Be stranded on **AN ISLAND ALONE**
or **WITH SOMEONE YOU CAN'T STAND**?

Live on a **HOUSEBOAT** or in a **MOUNTAIN CABIN**?

Go **DEEP-SEA DIVING** or **CAVE-EXPLORING**?

Be an **EAGLE** or a **WHALE**?

Build a **SNOWMAN** or a **SANDCASTLE**?

Photograph **BIGFOOT** or a **UFO**?

CIRCLE YOUR ANSWER THEN COMPARE WITH YOUR FRIEND.

WOULD YOU RATHER...

Have a **MERMAID TAIL** or **FAIRY WINGS**?

Go **SURFING** or **SOAK IN A HOT TUB**?

Have a **CLOAK OF INVISIBILITY** or
the **ABILITY TO READ MINDS**?

Explore the deep sea or outer space?

Play a **VILLAIN** or a **HERO** in a film?

Marry someone very **WEALTHY** or very **GOOD-LOOKING**?

Time-travel 50 years into t**HE FUTURE**
or 50 years into **THE PAST**?

Be stranded on **AN ISLAND ALONE**
or **WITH SOMEONE YOU CAN'T STAND**?

Live on a **HOUSEBOAT** or in a **MOUNTAIN CABIN**?

Go **DEEP-SEA DIVING** or **CAVE-EXPLORING**?

Be an **EAGLE** or a **WHALE**?

Build a **SNOWMAN** or a **SANDCASTLE**?

Photograph **BIGFOOT** or a **UFO**?

Who is your favorite superhero? Why?

....
....
....
....
....
....
....
....
....
....
....

What appeal do those special powers hold for you?

....
....
....
....
....
....
....
....
....
....
....
....
....

Who is your favorite superhero? Why?

What appeal do those special powers hold for you?

You have all the resources you need to start a business. What would it be?

....
....
....
....
....
....
....
....
....
....
....

What would be fabulous about owning that business?

....
....
....
....
....
....
....
....
....
....
....
....

You have all the resources you need to start a business. What would it be?

What would be fabulous about owning that business?

HOW WELL DO YOU KNOW YOUR BESTIE?

In a big city

Deep in the woods

On a farm

In a small town

In a foreign country

Teacher

Engineer

Artist

Scientist

Accountant

Farmhouse

Cabin

Mansion

Apartment

Modern house

CIRCLE THE ANSWER THAT BEST FITS YOUR FRIEND, THEN CHECK EACH OTHER'S WORK!

WHERE COULD YOU IMAGINE YOUR FRIEND LIVING IN THE FUTURE?

In a big city

Deep in the woods

On a farm

In a small town

In a foreign country

WHICH CAREER DO YOU THINK YOUR FRIEND WOULD MOST ENJOY?

Teacher

Engineer

Artist

Scientist

Accountant

WHAT TYPE OF HOME WOULD BEST SUIT YOUR FRIEND?

Farmhouse

Cabin

Mansion

Apartment

Modern house

What's hobby would you like to get paid to do?

Share a saying that motivates you.

Who serves as a role model for your career goals?

When are the best hours of the day for you to be creative?

Where do you go to regroup and recharge your batteries?

What would you do with an unexpected influx of cash?

If you were elected leader of your country,
what is the first action you would take?

How would you work to improve the lives of citizens?

If you were elected president,
what is the first action you would take?

How would you work to improve the lives of citizens?

BETTER TOGETHER

Everything is better with

you two as a team. These

invitations to reflect,

prompts for action, and

ideas for fun adventures

will make you super

thankful for a best friend

who just gets you.

What would be your absolute perfect day with your friend?

What would be your absolute perfect day with your friend?

How often do you get together with your BFF?

....
....
....
....
....
....
....
....
....
....
....
....

Is that enough time or do you wish you had more?

....
....
....
....
....
....
....
....
....
....
....
....
....

How often do you get together with your BFF?

Is that enough time or do you wish you had more?

How I know you really get me:

....
....
....
....
....
....
....
....
....

How I know you really get me:

....
....
....
....
....
....
....
....
....
....

ADVENTURES TO TRY

MAKE A [✓] CHECKMARK NEXT TO EACH THING YOU'D LIKE TO TRY. IF YOU'D BOTH LIKE TO TAKE ON THE ADVENTURE, MARK IT IN THE "TO SHARE" COLUMN.

	☆	SHARE	☼
ROCK CLIMBING			
STAND-UP PADDLE BOARDING			
COOKING CLASS			
ZIP-LINING			
ESCAPE ROOM			
CAMPING			
KARAOKE			
SPONTANEOUS DAY TRIP			
FOOD TOUR			
TRAMPOLINE PARK			

What does your bestie do to make you laugh?

....
....
....
....
....
....
....
....
....
....
....
....
....

Have you two ever cracked up at an inappropriate moment?

....
....
....
....
....
....
....
....
....
....
....
....
....

What does your bestie do to make you laugh?

Have you two ever cracked up at an inappropriate moment?

How can you help your friend achieve goals they have set?

....
....
....
....
....
....
....
....
....
....
....

How can your friend help you reach your goals?

....
....
....
....
....
....
....
....
....
....
....
....

How can you help your friend achieve goals they have set?

How can your friend help you reach your goals?

What is one thing you'd like to do with your BFF in the coming year? Plan it!

What is one thing you'd like to do with your BFF in the coming year? Plan it!

Map a walking tour of your town or other local spot. What are the points of interest? How many fun places to visit, eat at, or shop can you include? Take your friend on the tour.

Map a walking tour of your town or other local spot. What are the points of interest? How many fun places to visit, eat at, or shop can you include? Take your friend on the tour.

What has your friend done that you are most proud of?

How can you support your BFF in achieving more such
moments in the future?

What has your friend done that you are most proud of?

How can you support your BFF in achieving more such
moments in the future?

You and your bestie are starring together in a buddy movie.
What's the main plot?

....

....

....

....

....

....

Draw the movie poster.

You and your bestie are starring together in a buddy movie.
What's the main plot?

....

....

....

....

....

....

Draw the movie poster.

Why do you think you and your best friend get along so well?

....

....

....

....

....

....

....

....

....

....

....

....

Is there a secret to your friendship?

....

....

....

....

....

....

....

....

....

....

....

Why do you think you and your best friend get along so well?

Is there a secret to your friendship?

10 Things That Are Better When Shared

1.

2.

3.

4.

5.

6.

7.

8.

9.

10.

1.

2.

3.

4.

5.

6.

7.

8.

9.

10.

FRIENDSHIP BUILDERS

WHAT CAN YOU DO TOGETHER TO SPREAD THE
LOVE IN YOUR COMMUNITY? USE DIFFERENT
COLORS TO CIRCLE YOUR CHOICES, THEN MAKE A
PLAN TO DO THE ACTIVITIES YOU'VE BOTH CIRCLED.

VOLUNTEER AT A FOOD PANTRY

PLANT A COMMUNITY GARDEN

ORGANIZE A STUDY OR HOMEWORK HELP GROUP

HOST A PARK CLEANUP

HOST A PARK CLEANUP

OFFER CHILD CARE DURING PTA MEETINGS

DO YARDWORK FOR AN OLDER NEIGHBOR

HELP WITH SOCIAL MEDIA AT A LOCAL ORGANIZATION

COLLECT AND DONATE SCHOOL SUPPLIES

START A LITTLE FREE LIBRARY

SEW OR KNIT HATS AND MITTENS FOR PEOPLE IN SHELTERS

ORGANIZE A CLOTHING SWAP

MAKE HOLIDAY GIFTS FOR SENIORS IN CARE FACILITIES

VOLUNTEER AT AN ANIMAL SHELTER

ATTEND COMMUNITY MEETINGS AND
GET INVOLVED IN LOCAL ISSUES

SUNSHINE ON GRAY DAYS

Even on the roughest days,
your friendship acts as a
cheery sunbeam. And while
the two of you may have
your spats, you know how
to pick up, move on, and say
all is forgiven—that's why
you'll always be BFFs!

How does your BFF cheer you up when you're down?

....
....
....
....
....
....
....
....
....
....
....
....

Describe a time your friend was there when you really needed a boost.

....
....
....
....
....
....
....
....
....
....
....
....
....
....

How does your BFF cheer you up when you're down?

Describe a time your friend was there when you really needed a boost.

Your friend has a broken heart from a recent romance gone wrong.
What advice do you give?

What would you never say?

Your friend has a broken heart from a recent romance gone wrong.
What advice do you give?

What would you never say?

Write about a time you couldn't have gotten through the day without your best friend by your side.

Write about a time you couldn't have gotten through the day without your best friend by your side.

When is it hard to be a good friend?

When is it hard to be a good friend?

A time we got in trouble together was . . .

....

....

....

....

....

....

....

Our biggest fight was . . .

....

....

....

....

....

....

....

The biggest mistake we've made was . . .

....

....

....

....

....

....

....

A time we got in trouble together was . . .

....
....
....
....
....
....
....

Our biggest fight was . . .

....
....
....
....
....
....
....

The biggest mistake we've made was . . .

....
....
....
....
....
....
....

Have you ever broken a promise to a friend?

....
....
....
....
....
....
....
....
....
....
....

When might it be necessary?

....
....
....
....
....
....
....
....
....
....
....
....

Have you ever broken a promise to a friend?

When might it be necessary?

You see your friend about to make what you think is a gigantic mistake.
How do you approach a conversation with them about it?

You see your friend about to make what you think is a gigantic mistake.
How do you approach a conversation with them about it?

STRESS RELIEF

STRESSORS

1

2

3

STRESS RELIEVERS

1

2

3

NAME THREE THINGS THAT STRESS YOU OUT.
THEN LIST THREE WAYS YOU RELIEVE YOUR STRESS.

STRESSORS

1

2

3

STRESS RELIEVERS

1

2

3

Is there anything your best friend could do that
you would find unforgivable?

....
....
....
....
....
....
....

Why would that be so hard to excuse?

....
....
....
....
....
....
....

What would a heartfelt apology look like?

....
....
....
....
....
....
....

Is there anything your best friend could do that
you would find unforgivable?

Why would that be so hard to excuse?

What would a heartfelt apology look like?

HOW WELL DO YOU KNOW YOUR BESTIE?

THE PERSON YOUR
BFF FIGHTS WITH
MOST:

FAVORITE COMFORT
FOOD:

ONE THING THAT GETS
YOUR FRIEND DOWN:

WRITES THANK-YOU
NOTES TO RELATIVES
FOR GIFTS–
YES OR NO:

BEST LITTLE PICK-ME-
UP GIFT:

HIGH STRUNG OR
EASYGOING:

USUALLY FIRST TO
APOLOGIZE AFTER AN
ARGUMENT–YES OR NO:

A SAYING YOUR FRIEND
FINDS INSPIRATIONAL
DURING ROUGH TIMES:

MORE LIKELY TO
DROWN SORROWS
IN ICE CREAM OR
CHOCOLATE:

THINKS WHITE LIES
ARE OKAY IN CERTAIN
CIRCUMSTANCES–YES
OR NO:

FILL IN THE BLANKS, THEN CHECK EACH OTHER'S WORK!

THE PERSON YOUR
BFF FIGHTS WITH
MOST:

FAVORITE COMFORT
FOOD:

ONE THING THAT GETS
YOUR FRIEND DOWN:

WRITES THANK-YOU
NOTES TO RELATIVES
FOR GIFTS—
YES OR NO:

BEST LITTLE PICK-ME-
UP GIFT:

HIGH STRUNG OR
EASYGOING:

USUALLY FIRST TO
APOLOGIZE AFTER AN
ARGUMENT—YES OR NO:

A SAYING YOUR FRIEND
FINDS INSPIRATIONAL
DURING ROUGH TIMES:

MORE LIKELY TO
DROWN SORROWS
IN ICE CREAM OR
CHOCOLATE:

THINKS WHITE LIES
ARE OKAY IN CERTAIN
CIRCUMSTANCES—YES
OR NO:

What is the best way to settle disagreements or conflicts?

....
....
....
....
....
....
....
....
....
....
....
....

Why does it work well?

....
....
....
....
....
....
....
....
....
....
....
....
....

What is the best way to settle disagreements or conflicts?

Why does it work well?

Have you ever regretted something you said to your friend?
What was it and why did you regret it?

How did you remedy the situation, if you did at all?

Have you ever regretted something you said to your friend?
What was it and why did you regret it?

How did you remedy the situation, if you did at all?

Do you let your friend know when you need something?
Why or why not?

Do you let your friend know when you need something?
Why or why not?

CHANGES

With time, we
inevitably grow and
change—and so does
the world around us.
Look forward with joy
and anticipate the
changes that might lie
ahead in your life and
your friendship.

How has your friendship changed over the past year?

....

....

....

....

....

....

....

....

....

....

....

What do you think the coming year will bring?

....

....

....

....

....

....

....

....

....

....

....

....

How has your friendship changed over the past year?

What do you think the coming year will bring?

If you were moving across the country,
what would you miss most about your friend?

....
....
....
....
....
....
....
....
....
....
....

How do you think the distance would affect your friendship?

....
....
....
....
....
....
....
....
....
....
....
....
....
....

If you were moving across the country,
what would you miss most about your friend?

....
....
....
....
....
....
....
....
....
....
....
....

How do you think the distance would affect your friendship?

....
....
....
....
....
....
....
....
....
....
....
....
....

I like change because . . .

....

....

....

....

....

....

....

New situations scare me because . . .

....

....

....

....

....

....

I cope with change by . . .

....

....

....

....

....

....

....

I like change because . . .

....

....

....

....

....

....

....

New situations scare me because . . .

....

....

....

....

....

....

....

I cope with change by . . .

....

....

....

....

....

....

....

Where do you hope to be five years from now?

....
....
....
....
....
....
....

Ten?

....
....
....
....
....
....
....

Fifteen?

....
....
....
....
....
....
....

Where do you hope to be five years from now?

....

....

....

....

....

....

....

Ten?

....

....

....

....

....

....

....

Fifteen?

....

....

....

....

....

....

....

If you could change one thing in your life, what would it be?

How would life be better?

174

If you could change one thing in your life, what would it be?

How would life be better?

What do you think the world will be like when you are sixty-five years old?

....

....

....

....

....

....

....

How will technological progress and other advances make life easier
in the future?

....

....

....

....

....

....

....

What might be more difficult?

....

....

....

....

....

....

....

What do you think the world will be like when you are sixty-five years old?

How will technological progress and other advances make life easier in the future?

What might be more difficult?

If you could choose your BFF's first name, what would it be? Why?

What new name would you choose for yourself if you could, and why?

If you could choose your BFF's first name, what would it be? Why?

What new name would you choose for yourself if you could, and why?

How will you stay connected to your BFF as you get older?

How will you stay connected to your BFF as you get older?

JUST FOR FUN

Unleash your own
quirky opinions and
learn more about your
bestie's outlook with
entertaining quizzes,
lists, and questions!

Would you like to be famous? For what?

What might the downside be?

Would you like to be famous? For what?

What might the downside be?

LIKE & DISLIKE

	LIKE	DISLIKE
ICE CREAM FLAVOR		
DAY OF THE WEEK		
SPECTATOR SPORT		
TAKE-OUT FOOD		
SONG		
VEGETABLE		
SCENT		
BOOK CHARACTER		
VIDEO GAME		
FLOWER		

FOR EACH ENTRY, WRITE A TYPE YOU LIKE AND ONE YOU DISLIKE.

	LIKE	DISLIKE
ICE CREAM FLAVOR		
DAY OF THE WEEK		
SPECTATOR SPORT		
TAKE-OUT FOOD		
SONG		
VEGETABLE		
SCENT		
BOOK CHARACTER		
VIDEO GAME		
FLOWER		

Have you ever had a brush with the paranormal (had an experiences that is beyond scientific explanation)? If so, what was it? If not, do you believe in ghosts, magic, or other things outside our understanding of the natural world?

Have you ever had a brush with the paranormal (had an experiences that is beyond scientific explanation)? If so, what was it? If not, do you believe in ghosts, magic, or other things outside our understanding of the natural world?

What is the best thing about social media?

....

....

....

....

....

....

....

....

....

....

....

....

What is the worst thing?

....

....

....

....

....

....

....

....

....

....

....

What is the best thing about social media?

What is the worst thing?

Design a graphic T-shirt for your BFF. You can include a word or saying, a symbol, a drawing, or any other artwork that represents your friend.

Design a graphic T-shirt for your BFF. You can include a word or saying, a symbol, a drawing, or any other artwork that represents your friend.

What five things do you always have with you?
Why do you like to have each of these items on hand?

1.
....
....
....

2.
....
....
....

3.
....
....
....

4.
....
....
....

5.
....
....
....

What five things do you always have with you?
Why do you like to have each of these items on hand?

1.

2.

3.

4.

5.

What is your favorite smell? Why? What memories does it bring back?

What is your favorite smell? Why? What memories does it bring back?

HOW WELL DO YOU KNOW YOUR BESTIE?

SPRING OR FALL?

SWIMMING IN A LAKE/OCEAN OR SWIMMING IN A POOL?

EARLY MORNINGS OR LATE NIGHTS?

FLANNEL SHEETS OR SILKY SHEETS?

LONG HIKE OR LAZY PICNIC?

DARK CHOCOLATE OR MILK CHOCOLATE?

PINK OR BLACK?

READING A ROMANCE OR A MYSTERY?

COKE OR PEPSI?

PLANNED PARTY OR SURPRISE PARTY?

ROSES OR TULIPS?

PUMPKIN PIE OR APPLE PIE?

SEESAW OR SWINGS?

SOUP OR SALAD?

THEME PARK OR ZOO?

TOWN OR COUNTRY?

HOT CIDER OR HOT CHOCOLATE?

AFRICAN SAFARI OR TRIP TO PARIS?

CHEESEBURGER OR PIZZA?

COMPUTER CODING OR ART PROJECT?

OUTDOORSY OR INDOORSY?

SUMMER OLYMPICS OR WINTER OLYMPICS?

PEANUT BUTTER OR NUTELLA?

PUPPIES OR KITTENS?

SALTY OR SWEET SNACKS?

CIRCLE THE ANSWER THAT BEST FITS YOUR FRIEND, THEN CHECK EACH OTHER'S WORK!

SPRING OR FALL?

SWIMMING IN A LAKE/OCEAN OR SWIMMING IN A POOL?

EARLY MORNINGS OR LATE NIGHTS?

FLANNEL SHEETS OR SILKY SHEETS?

LONG HIKE OR LAZY PICNIC?

DARK CHOCOLATE OR MILK CHOCOLATE?

PINK OR BLACK?

READING A ROMANCE OR A MYSTERY?

COKE OR PEPSI?

PLANNED PARTY OR SURPRISE PARTY?

ROSES OR TULIPS?

PUMPKIN PIE OR APPLE PIE?

SEESAW OR SWINGS?

SOUP OR SALAD?

THEME PARK OR ZOO?

TOWN OR COUNTRY?

HOT CIDER OR HOT CHOCOLATE?

AFRICAN SAFARI OR TRIP TO PARIS?

CHEESEBURGER OR PIZZA?

COMPUTER CODING OR ART PROJECT?

OUTDOORSY OR INDOORSY?

SUMMER OLYMPICS OR WINTER OLYMPICS?

PEANUT BUTTER OR NUTELLA?

PUPPIES OR KITTENS?

SALTY OR SWEET SNACKS?

What is the first thing you do when you get up in the morning?

....
....
....
....
....
....
....
....
....
....
....
....

What's the last thing you do before bed?

....
....
....
....
....
....
....
....
....
....
....
....
....

What is the first thing you do when you get up in the morning?

What's the last thing you do before bed?

What gives you confidence we will be best friends forever?